C000253503

COUNSELLING
CANCER
PATIENTS

COUNSELLING CANCER PATIENTS

A MUST READ!

ETHEL K. ZIMBA SIWILA

PARTRIDGE

To order additional copies of this book, contact
Toll Free 0800 990 914 (South Africa)
+44 20 3014 3997 (outside South Africa)
orders.africa@partridgepublishing.com

www.partridgepublishing.com/africa

TABLE OF CONTENTS

This book is dedicated to cancer
patients and their families.

ACKNOWLEDGEMENT

First and foremost I am grateful to the Almighty God for enabling me to come up with this book without whom it was totally going to be impossible to accomplish. To him be the glory, honour, and praise.

I wish to thank my husband Boster Dearson Siwila for his spiritual and material support; "Dada am grateful". My children too for their encouragement.

My gratitude go to the members of staff at the Cancer Diseases Hospital for their guidance and knowledge contributed to the writing of this book; Dr S. Msadabwe – Oncologist, and Acting Senior Medical Superintendent, Dr Catherine Mwaba – Oncologist, Matron Maliti Biemba, Mrs Emily Lishimpi – Social Worker and the entire Social Work unit. Mrs Wila Z. Chinyeka - Dietician and Mr Gilbert Phiri the information officer as well as Mrs Patience M. Simuunza the Palliative Care nurse.

I wish to thank Dr Changala M. - Lecturer at the University of Zambia for editing this work despite his busy schedule. He gave me the confidence to go ahead. And all the Lecturers in the Department of Adult and Extension Studies –Mr

Moonga, Mr Sichula, Dr Mbozi, Mr Ngoma, Mr Mwansa and Mr Luchembe to mention but a few. Out of the many assignments they used to give us, I acquired the skill and interest to write.

I am as well grateful to Dr Neo Simutanyi: Director - Centre for Policy Dialogue for stirring the skill to write out of the assignments he used to give us during my attachment period with my friend Nyembezi Kasaro.

CHAPTER 1

WHY COUNSEL CANCER PATIENTS?

A diagnosis of cancer may leave patients feeling helpless and out of control. Every cancer patient faces the fear of recurrence, death, stigma and the need for having hope throughout their life time. As such, there is a common language that can be used to counsel all patients of cancer; from every corner of the earth although, there may be some differences in terms of culture and values. The support of a counsellor may help to give hope and help one to cope with the psychosocial impact of the disease. This makes counselling an important aspect of treatment for the patients and their loved ones; especially today that the illness has become a generative theme. The Zambia Counselling Council (1999) define counselling as a therapeutic and helping relationship through which individuals are helped to define goals, make decisions and resolve problems related to personal, educational, health and psychosocial concerns. The aim of counselling is to improve the client's capacity and ability to cope with and manage their presenting problems in order to enable them live a more personally satisfying life. Through this process, the client can develop a better understanding of themselves, including their thought patterns, feelings, and behaviours, and the ways in which these may have been problematic in their lives and explore ways of dealing with such problems or feelings. Counselling provides an opportunity to change the unhelpful patterns and to examine how to tap into the client's existing resources or to develop new ones to allow for better, more satisfying emotional and social functioning. Moreover, it helps clients to see things more clearly, possibly from a different view point. Cancer has an impact on the whole person, as such, it needs to be handled holistically for better outcomes. This calls for the consideration of counselling as an important aspect in cancer treatment.

Impact of Cancer on an Individual

Cancer is likely to be a frightening and life altering disease, especially if the diagnosed type of cancer grows quickly or has already spread to other parts of the body. A person diagnosed with an advanced stage of cancer may begin to think about and possibly fear the approaching end of life. Fear of death has all sorts of complications for living. Some areas that particularly come to mind are commitments. Shall I commit myself to a new job? Shall I commit myself to long term things in life? What about future planning? The real horror of cancer is not knowing whether one is going to live or die. Moreover, those who have undergone treatment with no evidence of the disease are still very frightened of reoccurrences. Many may fear becoming unable to work and losing their income. As strong as those cancer survivors may be, many are also afraid and confused. They want help to figure out what their next steps will be. They need to be helped to deal with elements such as managing stress, and healthy living through counselling (Docksai, 2015). Cancer impacts on individuals at various aspects. These are as discussed below:

- **Psychological Impact**.

This is the effect of a cancer diagnosis on the mind of an individual. It brings about unique feelings, emotions, thoughts and attitudes that can only be understood by the affected individual. Individuals go into denial, depression, anger and experience stress and anxiety as well as fear and worry. (National Cancer Institute, 2015). The fear of death is also exhibited in the attitude and behaviour. It is therefore the duty of a counsellor to interpret these feelings as portrayed by the client and intervene as this might lead to a premature loss of life because the client can easily give up.

- **Physical Impact.**

These are physical changes that come with cancer. The invasive nature of this disease and its aggressive treatment produce distressing physical symptoms, such as pain, nausea, anorexia and fatigue as well as weight loss (Farber, Weinerman and Kuypers, 1985). Some chemotherapy drugs make patients lose hair on the whole body making them bald. Furthermore, some breast cancer patients and others with uterine, cervical, prostate and eye cancers have their affected organs removed; a situation that make their physical appearance different from other people.

There are also skin changes for patients undergoing both chemotherapy and radiotherapy. Some of the changes are not permanent; they disappear with time. Breast cancer patients, are given artificial breasts to help maintain the shape together with those with amputated limbs. The counsellor in this case needs to reassure the patients and help them adjust further to the situation in order for them to maintain their self-esteem and worthiness. Pain is another problem faced by cancer patients.

- **Pain**

Pain can be physical and emotional. Physical pain is what the patient says hurts. It can be acute or chronic According to Moyniham (2014) not everyone with cancer experiences pain, but one out of three people undergoing cancer treatment does. Patients with advanced cancer have a chance of experiencing cancer pain more than others. If someone has pain, he or she might not be able to take part in the normal day to day activities. They may have trouble sleeping and eating; they may be irritable with the people they love, be frustrated, sad and even angry.

Pain can be caused by a tumour growing in an organ. If it spreads to the bones or other organs, it may put pressure on nerves and damage them causing pain. Additionally, if a tumour spreads or grows around the spinal cord, it can cause a compression of the spinal cord, which eventually leads to severe pain or paralysis if not treated. Pain can as well be a side effect of treatment like, surgery, chemotherapy or radiotherapy. Or it can result from causes not related to the cancer at all (American Society of Clinical Oncology, 2014)

Pain should never be accepted as a normal part of cancer. All pain can be treated, and most pain can be controlled or relieved. When pain is controlled, people can sleep and eat better, enjoy being with family and friends and continue with their work and hobbies (American Cancer Society 2015). The counsellor dealing with a patient in pain has to refer that patient to an oncologist through an oncology or palliative care nurse for appropriate pain assessment and management. Emotional pain affects the mind and brings about all kinds of worries, fears, anxiety and stress. A patient experiencing this pain just like the physical one; will be irritable, sad, withdrawn and will have no appetite. This type of pain cannot be treated with drugs but with counselling.

- **Socio – Economic Impact**

Cancer diseases have an impact on the social and economic wellbeing of the patient as an individual and the family as a whole. It is an illness that demands long periods of treatment and management. Additionally, the illness and the treatment make the patient lose the strength to work to make ends meet; the patient and the family are constrained financially. This situation impacts on the economy of the nations as well. The impact is worse if it is the mother who is sick because of her role in the home. The children lack motherly care and suffer as a result. Some women have reportedly been abandoned by their husbands due to cancer. However, some women too leave their husbands because of cancer. Furthermore, some women complain of their husbands abandoning them for other women, if there is a child with cancer in the home.

Besides, society stigmatises those with cancer for fear of contracting the disease due to lack of knowledge. Others are abandoned due to bad odour with advanced disease and fungating tumours. In such situations counselling is necessary to educate the patient and the family members on the illness and what is required of them. It should be mentioned that life does not end at diagnosis. Instead, diagnosis is the beginning of the understanding of the 'new' normal. This may help the client to remain positive and be productive as far as their health can allow.

Cancer patients need to be counselled to reduce the impact the disease has on their lives and the entire society. Cancer impact can lead to loss of function, non-adherent to treatment and premature loss of life. As such, all cancer patients need to be counselled alongside their routine treatment. Through counselling, patients are educated on the disease, types of treatment and the side effects as well as everything that comes with the disease like; the fear of recurrences, stigma and the fear of death. The patients' questions are also answered accordingly, depending on the counsellor's knowledge and expertise. If the counsellor is not knowledgeable on the matter in question, it is prudent to refer the patient to other people who may be more knowledgeable. Hope is also given for the patient to have something to look forward, which helps in dealing with negative thoughts that could otherwise bring them down. Furthermore, counselling helps families to come together and understand what their loved one is going through and so help them take good care of themselves and the affected family member.

Worldwide Cancer Burden

Cancer is the disease that has affected people of all races and colour worldwide covering both the developed and developing countries; it is a common disease in all nations of the world. It`s impact on an individual and society is the same. The World Health Organisation (2015) has pointed out the worldwide key facts about cancer. These are:

- Cancer figures are among the leading cases of morbidity and mortality worldwide, with approximately 14 million new cases and 8.2 million cancer related deaths in 2012. According to Evert (2010) cancer is the leading cause of death in Americans under the age of 85, and the second leading cause of death in older Americans.
- The number of new cases is expected to rise by about 70% over the next 2 decades.
- Among men, the 5 most common sites of cancer diagnosed in 2012 were lung, prostate, colorectum, stomach and liver.
- Among women, the 5 most common sites diagnosed were breast, colorectum, lung, cervix and stomach.
- Around one third of cancer deaths are due to the 5 leading behavioural and dietary risks: high body mass index, low fruit and vegetable intake, lack of physical activity, tobacco use and alcohol. Tobacco causes around 20% of global cancer deaths and around 70% of global lung cancer deaths.
- More than 60% of world`s total new annual cases occur in Africa, Asia and Central and Southern

America. These regions account for 70% of the world's cancer deaths.

- It is expected that annual cancer cases will rise from 14 million in 2012 to 22 within the next 2 decades.

Cancer Burden in Africa

According to Jemal, e tal (2012) cancer is an emerging public health problem in Africa. About 715,000 new cancer cases and 542,000 cancer deaths occurred in 2008 on the continent with these numbers expected to double in the next 20 years simply because of the aging and growth of the population as well as increased prevalence of risk factors associated with economic transition, including smoking, obesity, physical inactivity and reproductive behaviours. The other issue of concern as regards cancer in Africa is the late detection of the disease.

In Zambia, just like many other African countries, patients often seek medical attention late when the cancer has already advanced.

The contributing factor to this is the nature of the disease. It remains silent with no symptoms at the beginning; the symptoms appear as the disease progresses. This is why emphasis is being put on routine medical check-ups, so that if there be any cancer developing, it is detected early and treated for better outcomes. Furthermore, due to lack of knowledge in the community, some symptoms are ignored or mistaken for other illnesses. Even amongst medical practitioners, cancer is the last illness to consider for a diagnosis. It is when other options prove futile that a diagnosis of cancer is considered. "A majority of cancers in Africa are diagnosed at an advanced stage because of lack of screening and early detection services, as well as limited awareness of early signs and symptoms of cancer among the public and health care providers" (American Cancer Society, 2011). Additionally, it is common practice in Africa for an individual to seek treatment from a traditional healer first before going to the hospital. A study conducted in Egypt, Nigeria, Ghana, Kenya and Libya by Donkor (2015) entitled "Factors contributing to late presentation of breast cancer patients in Africa", revealed that; Africans have different beliefs which are rooted in their cultural forces, individual experiences and perceptions. Many cultures in Africa associate cancer with a supernatural rather than a biological basis. Symptoms of cancer are attributed to a curse, bewitching, God or god`s punishment due to personal or family atrocity or demons which can lead to death. Hence, individuals prefer to rely on their faith in sorcerers, witch doctors, herbalists, priest/pastors and other spiritualists to treat cancer. The delays in seeking medical attention make the disease advance and impact negatively on an individual and the family.

The Cancer Burden in Zambia

Zambia has in the recent past seen an unprecedented rise in cancer incident rates. This is an indication that more vigorous efforts towards fighting cancer need to be instituted. Awareness campaigns and counselling of already affected patients are some of the efforts that should be doubled given that treatment is available with the existence of a Cancer Diseases Hospital. The hospital is catering for the whole nation with a total population of 13,092,666 broken down as 49.3 percent (6,454,647) of males and 50.7 percent (6,638,019) of females according to the 2010 national census (Central Statistical Office as quoted in the Zambia National Cancer Registry Report, 2012).

The Top Ten Cancers in Zambia

The figures below show the top ten cancers among the males and females in Zambia according to the Zambia National Registry cancer registration of 2008 to 2012.

Males

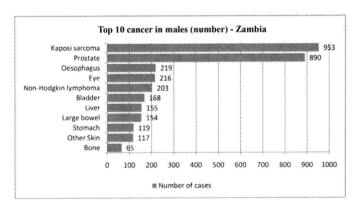

Source: Zambia National Cancer Registry.

Females

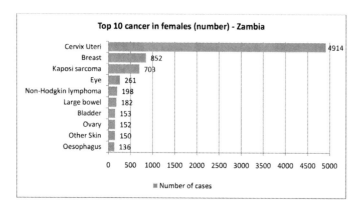

Source: Zambia National Cancer Registry.

Among the males, Kaposis Sarcoma 953 and prostate 890 cancers were the most commonly diagnosed cancers, followed by oesophageal 219 and eye cancer 216. As for females; cervical 4914 and breast 852 cancers were the most commonly diagnosed followed by kaposis sarcoma 703 and eye cancer 261.

Childhood Cancers

Children in Zambia are also affected by cancer. There are childhood cancers and those that common in all age groups. The common cancers among the Zambian boys and girls aged 0-14 are shown in the table below:

Childhood cancer registrations in 2008-2012 for aged 0-14 by cancer site and sex

Cancer type	Boys	Girls	Total
Kaposi sarcoma	47	35	82
Nephroblastoma	15	24	39
Retinoblastoma	16	21	37
Malignant lymphoma, non-Hodgkin	19	13	32
Burkitt lymphoma	17	8	25
Osteosarcoma	8	9	17
Hodgkin lymphoma	13	3	16
Astrocytoma	6	3	9

Source: Zambia National Cancer Registry.

The above table shows the number of childhood cancer cases for boys and girls aged 0-14 for the period 2008-2012 in Zambia. It shows that the proportion of cases registered in boys were slightly higher for most cancer types compared to the number of cases in girls. Kaposis sarcoma is the highest in both sexes followed by lymphomas in boys. Nephroblastoma and retinoblastoma are the next highest cases of cancers affecting girls in Zambia.

According to the latest cancer information from the Zambia Cancer Diseases Hospital (2015), cancer cases seen at the hospital are increasing each year

Below is the figure showing cancer cases since 2006 when the Hospital was opened up to 2015.

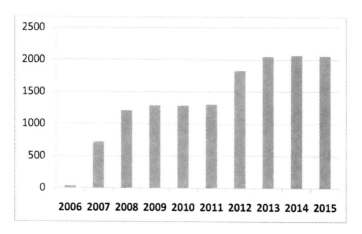

Source: Cancer Diseases Hospital

. In 2006 thirty five patients were attended to, in 2007 there were 719 patients; in 2008 there were 1204 patients while in 2009 the hospital recorded a total of 1285 patients. In 2010 there was a record of 1282 patients; in 2011 there were1302 patients; 2012 recorded 1828 patients; 2013 recorded 2049 and 2065 patients were recorded in 2014. The year 2015 saw a slight reduction in the number of cases compared to the previous 4 years in which there was a steady increase. 2015 recorded a total of 2058 patients. The grand total for all the patients seen at the cancer hospital since inception to 2015 December was 13, 827.

The above figures are posing a huge challenge worldwide to counsellors and governments making the need for counselling an integral part of treatment as a way of maintaining the social, physical and psychological functioning of society.

This will enable cancer patients to lead normal lives as far as possible and help reduce the cancer burden on society. The patients can be treated with all the available treatment modalities but without the psychotherapy through counselling, optimal therapy cannot be achieved because the mind that controls the whole body is left out. Therefore, counselling is necessary to give hope and help patients accept their condition as a 'new' normal and continue functioning for as long as time and health can allow. Counselling may help someone to develop a positive mental and emotional attitude towards their illness and have a fighting spirit to live longer and accomplish their goals in life.

Perhaps now the question that may be lingering in the mind of the reader could be` what then is cancer`? Chapter 2 gives out the details about cancer as regards what it is, its risk factors, signs and symptoms, treatment and side effects as well as its prevention strategies. This knowledge is important to the counsellors, patients, care givers and all the readers in understanding cancer as a disease.

CHAPTER 2

WHAT IS CANCER?

Cancer is the disease that starts in the cells of a human body. As taught in high School: a cell is a basic unit of life. Cancer has no specific cause but there factors that lead to individuals developing cancer in their life time. There are many types of cancers affecting different organs of the human body. A cancer is named after the organ it affects like cancer of the breast if it starts in the breast. It can start in the lungs, the breast, and the colon or even in the blood. It is a disease in which a group of abnormal cells grow uncontrollably by disregarding the normal rules of cell division. A cancer starts with changes in one cell or a small group of cells in the body. Some other types of cancer start from the blood like Leukaemia (Cancer Research UK, 2014).

Our bodies are made up of more than a hundred million cells. Cells have a control centre called a nucleus. Inside the nucleus are chromosomes made up of long strings of Deoxyribonucleic Acid (DNA). The DNA contains thousands of genes, which are coded messages that tell the cell how to behave. Genes make sure that cells grow and reproduce in an orderly and controlled way. Normal cells in the body grow and divide into new cells, and eventually die. Cancer begins when the DNA of a normal cell changes or is damaged as a result of exposure to risk factors and does not die but begin to make new cells that the body does not need. Some changes mean that the cell no longer understands its instructions and starts to grow out of control. The damaged cell then keeps multiplying and creates a tumour (National Cancer Institute, 2015).

Tumours can be benign or malignant. Benign tumours are not cancerous, thus they do not grow and spread like cancerous ones. Malignant tumours, on the other hand are cancerous, they grow and spread to other areas of the body. Some cancers grow and spread more quickly than others, and some cancers may not be as serious as others. Many types of cancers are treatable, partial and complete remission is also possible. Cancer may return at any time, a fact that may cause continued anxiety or worry even in those individuals who experience complete remission (National Cancer Institute, 2015).

Cancer Risk Factors

It is usually not possible to know exactly why one person develops cancer and another does not. But research has shown that certain factors, called risk factors, may increase a person's chances of suffering from cancer. The risk factors as considered in this book are; age, lifestyle and the environment, infections as well as genetic factors.

- **Age Related Factors**

Although cancer can occur in persons of every age, it is common among the aging population. The incidence of the following cancers increases with age; breast, colorectal, prostate and lung. This is because of age related alterations in the immune system, accumulation of random genetic mutations or life time carcinogen exposure, hormonal alterations or exposure and long life spans (Hejmadi, 2014).

- **Lifestyle and the Environment**

This is as a result of things such as:

- Smoking.
- Excessive alcohol consumption.
- Unhealthy eating habits.
- Lack of regular exercise
- Exposure to chemicals and Radiation.

- **Infections**

The risk of cancer is also increased by infectious agents including viruses like Hepatitis B Virus (HBV) causing Hepatocellular Carcinoma and the Human Papilloma Virus (HPV) which increases the risk of cervical cancer. The Human Immunodeficiency Virus (HIV) increase the risk of nasopharyngeal cancer and kaposis sarcoma. Bacteria such as Helicobacter pylori increase the risk of stomach cancers (Hejmadi, 2014).

- **Genetic Factors**

Some cancers like cancer of the breast, ovary, prostate, bowel, kidney, melanoma, pancreas and retinoblastoma as well as thyroid may be caused by abnormal genes that are passed from generation to generation (National Cancer Institute, 2015).

Signs and Symptoms of Cancer

Signs and symptoms of cancer differ depending on the type of cancer that one is suffering from. The following are the signs and symptoms according to the National Cancer Institute (2015)

- A new or an abnormal lump anywhere on the body.
- A sore that does not heal.
- Prolonged coughing or voice hoarseness.
- Prolonged constipation or diarrhoea
- Blood in the stool or urine.
- Difficulty/pain in passing urine or stool
- Bleeding or discharge.

These signs and symptoms may be as a result of other illnesses and not necessarily cancer. But it is important to go to the nearest clinic or hospital to be checked if one experiences any of the above mentioned signs and symptoms.

Cancer Treatment and Side Effects

Different types of cancer cells respond to treatment differently. Treatment of cancer often requires multiple approaches. These include surgery, radiation therapy, chemotherapy and hormonal therapy. The type and duration of treatment that one receives depends on the type of cancer and how advanced it is. But on average it takes months for one to complete the cancer treatment. Some may need more treatment if the cancer comes back or does not respond to the initial treatment (National Cancer Institute, 2015).

Chemotherapy is the type of cancer treatment that uses drugs to kill cancer cells. Radiation therapy uses high energy ionising radiation to shrink tumours and kill cancer cells. Furthermore, surgery is performed to remove the organ affected by the cancer; before it spreads to other organs. This is possible in the early stages of the disease. Sometimes surgery is performed to clean the wound caused by cancer if it is infected to aid in wound healing.

- **Goals of Cancer Treatment**

The goals of cancer treatment are to cure, control or offer palliation. Cure means that the cancer is destroyed; it goes away and does not come back. In this case, treatment is administered with curative intent. Although, cure may be the goal, it does not always work out that way. It often takes many years to know if a person's cancer is really cured. Cure may be possible when the cancer is in its early stage. According to the World Health Organisation (2014) cancer mortality can be reduced if cases are detected and treated early. It is for this reason that experts or health professionals encourage people to go for screening even when they have no symptoms for early detection.

The other goal is to control the disease if cure is not possible. The tumour cells are shrunk or stopped from growing and spreading. This can help the person with cancer feel better and live longer. In many cases, the cancer does not completely go away, but is controlled and managed as a chronic disease, much like heart disease or diabetes. In some cases, the cancer may even seem to have gone away for a while, but it is expected to come back.

When the cancer is at an advanced stage, meaning it is not under control and has spread from where it started to other parts of the body, treatment can be used to ease symptoms caused by the cancer. This is palliation. In this case, the goal is to improve the quality of life or help the person feel better (American Cancer Society, 2015).

• **Side Effects of Cancer Treatment**

Cancer treatments can cause side effects. These side effects vary from person to person, even among those receiving the same treatment. Therefore, before one starts treatment, it is important to ask the health care team what side effects one is likely to have (National Cancer Institute, 2015). Chemotherapy not only kills fast growing cancer cells, but also kills or slows the growth of healthy cells. This may lead to side effects such as mouth sores, nausea vomiting, hair loss, skin changes as well as fatigue. Additionally, chemotherapy can stop ones ovaries from working for a while, or possibly permanently depending on the type of the drug and dose and cause infertility (Cancer Research UK, 2015). Radiation therapy also damages normal cells leading to acute side effects like skin irritation or damage at regions exposed to the radiation beam. Examples include damage to the salivary glands or hair loss when the head or neck area is treated, or urinary problems when the lower abdomen is treated as well as nausea and vomiting, or even diarrhoea. These side effects disappear after one has finished treatment. Fatigue is a common side effect regardless of which part of the body is being treated. Late side effects include; fibrosis, damage to bowels causing diarrhoea and bleeding, memory loss, infertility and rarely a second cancer caused by radiation exposure (National Cancer Institute, 2015).

Surgery brings about changes and disabilities and malfunctions. Limbs (legs or arms) are amputated depending on the type of cancer. Affected Breasts, Eyes as well as internal organs are removed. Some patients begin to feed and breathe through tubes while others start using crutches or wheel chairs to walk. Breast cancer patients end up using artificial breasts to maintain the shape of the chest. However, some cancers cause deformities on their own. For example, an individual can have the nose destroyed by cancer of the nose.

Cancer Prevention

Cancer prevention is an action taken to lower the chances of getting cancer. By preventing cancer, the number of new cases of cancer is lowered reducing the burden of cancer and lowering the number of deaths caused by cancer. The knowledge of preventing cancer can be drawn from the risk factors. Most of the cancers are as a result of life style and can be prevented by adjusting or modifying the life style.

The following are the ways in which cancer can be prevented:

- Those who drink alcohol need to stop or drink in moderation as high alcohol consumption over time increases the risk of cancers of the mouth, throat, voice box and the liver.
- Giving up smoking or never smoking at all reduces the risk of developing cancer of the lungs, voice box, mouth, oesophagus, stomach, bladder, kidney, throat, pancreas and cervix.
- The Human Papilloma virus is sexually transmitted. It is a risk factor for cancers of the cervix, anus and penis. Hence, the need to practice safer sex and being cautious.
- Children who are not sexually active are vaccinated against the human papilloma virus to prevent cervical cancer in future.
- Some cancers are caused by chemicals and radiation. It is therefore, important to always follow health and safety guidelines when working with chemicals and ionising radiation.

- Early detection of precancerous conditions and the administration of medicines to treat the condition or to keep cancer from starting is another way to prevention. (National Cancer Institute, 2015).

On the other hand, eating a balanced diet that is low in fat and red meat and rich in fruits, vegetables and fibre can help reduce the risk of developing cancer. A healthy body weight reduces the risk of developing some cancers as well as regular exercising like walking, swimming, dancing, cycling or jogging. Additionally, our bodies need water as well to function properly; this calls for a daily routine water intake.

CHAPTER 3

BASIC COUNSELLING SKILLS

The counselling process is conducted using certain skills. There are many counselling skills that are used in counselling. This chapter shall consider the basic counselling skills. Basic counselling skills imply a repertoire of central counselling skills on which one can base his or her helping practice. The quality of the counsellor-client relationship is essential to successful helping encounters. Skills enhance the connection between the counsellor and the client (Online Counselling Service, 2016). In this chapter the skills that shall be discussed are communication, empathy, congruence and positive regard.

Communication Skills

Communication is the act of transferring information from one place to another, whether verbally, written and nonverbal. Being able to communicate effectively is the most important of all life skills. A counsellor should have good communication skills. These include: listening, clarifying, questioning and reflecting (Online Counselling Service, 2016).

- **Listening skill**

A counsellor must be a good and active listener. Active listening involves listening with all senses as well as giving full attention to the client otherwise the client may conclude that what he or she is talking about is not appreciated by the listener. Interest can be conveyed to the client by using both verbal and nonverbal messages such as maintaining eye contact, nodding your head and smiling as well as agreeing to encourage them to continue (HIV/AIDS Counselling, 2001). By providing this feedback the client will usually feel more at ease and, therefore, communicate more easily, openly and honestly. The counsellor should remain neutral and non- judgemental. This means trying not to take sides or form opinions, especially early in the conversation. It is also about patience, pauses and short periods of silence.

- **Clarifying and Clarification**

In communication, clarification involves offering back to the speaker the essential meaning, as understood by the listener, of what they have just said. Thereby, checking that the listener's understanding is correct and resolving any areas of confusion or misunderstanding. Clarification is important in many situations especially when what is being communicated is difficult in some way. Communication can be difficult for many reasons, perhaps sensitive emotions are being discussed or you are listening to some complex information or following instructions. The purpose of clarification is to ensure the listener's understanding of what the speaker has said is correct thereby, reducing misunderstanding. Clarification can involve asking questions or occasionally summarising what the client has said. Clarifying and clarification involves non-judgemental questioning, summarising and seeking feedback (HIV/AIDS Counselling, 2001). For effective communication it is essential that the counsellor and the client have both the same understanding of the discussion.

- **Questioning Skills and Techniques**

Gathering information is a basic human activity. We use information to learn, to help us solve problems, to aid our decision making process and to understand each other more clearly. Questioning is the key to gaining more information and without it interpersonal communications can fail. Questioning is fundamental to successful communication. Questions are asked in order to:

- obtain information
- help maintain control of a conversation
- express an interest in the other person
- clarify a point
- explore the personality and or difficulties the other person may have
- test knowledge
- encourage further thought(Online Counselling Service, 2016).

Being an effective communicator has to do with how questions are asked. Once the purpose of the question has been established, the counsellor should know what type of question should be asked, if the question is appropriate to the client, whether it is the right time to ask and know how the client will respond. Open ended questions are encouraged to be used than the closed ended ones. Asking open ended questions is a way of encouraging the client to talk more and give the counsellor the needed information. The most effective questioning starts with 'when', 'where', 'how' or 'why'. It encourages the speaker to be open and expand on their thoughts (HIV/AIDS Counselling, 2001).

- **Reflecting**

Reflecting refer to the counsellor's ability to communicate to the client his or her understanding of the client's concerns and perspectives at an emotional level. It is the process of paraphrasing and restating both the feelings and words of the client (HIV/AIDS Counselling, 2001). The counsellor has to reflect the content, feeling and meaning of what the client is saying. The most immediate part of a client's message is the content, in other words those aspects dealing with information, actions, events and experience, as verbalised by the client. According to Online Counselling Service (2016) reflecting content helps to give focus to the situation but, at the same time, it is also essential to reflect the feelings and emotions expressed in order to bring them into sharper focus. This helps the client to own and accept their own feelings, for quiet often a client may talk about him or herself as though they belong to someone else, for example using ``you feel guilty`` rather than ``I feel guilty``.

- **Mirroring**

Mirroring is a simple form of reflecting and involves repeating almost exactly what the speaker says. It should be short and simple. It is usually enough to just repeat key words or the last few words spoken. This shows you are trying to understand the speaker's terms of reference and acts as a prompt for him or her to continue. Be aware not to over mirror as this can become irritating and therefore distraction from the message (Online Counselling Service, 2016).

- **Paraphrasing**

Paraphrasing involves using other words to reflect what the speaker has said. Paraphrasing shows not only that you are listening, but that you are attempting to understand what the speaker is saying. When paraphrasing, it is of utmost importance that you do not introduce your own ideas or question the speaker's thoughts, feelings or actions. Your responses should be non-directive and non-judgemental (Online Counselling Service, 2016).

The purpose of reflecting is to:

- Allow the client to hear their own thoughts and to focus on what they say and feel.
- Show the client that you are trying to perceive the world as they see it and that you are doing your best to understand their messages.
- Encourage them to continue talking.

Empathy Skill

Empathy is awareness of the feelings and emotions of other people. It is a key element of emotional intelligence, the link between self and others. It is the way individuals understand what others are experiencing as if they were feeling it themselves. Empathy involves being able to understand the client's issues from their own frame of reference. The counsellor should be able to accurately reflect this understanding back to the client.

According to Egan (1994) empathy means entering the private perceptual world of the other and becoming thoroughly at home in it. It involves being sensitive, moment by moment, to the changing felt meanings which flow in this other person, to the fear or rage or tenderness or confusion or whatever that he or she is experiencing. It means temporarily living in the other's life, moving about in it delicately without making judgement.

Types of Empathy

Empathy can be:

- **Cognitive**

This means understanding someone's thoughts and emotions in a very rational rather than emotional sense.

- **Emotional**

This is also known as emotional contagion and is catching someone else`s feelings, so that you literally feel them too.

- **Compassionate**

Compassionate empathy is understanding someone`s feelings and taking appropriate action to help. It may not always be easy, or even possible, to empathise with others but, through good people skills and some imagination, we can work towards more empathetic feelings (Online Counselling Service, 2016)

Congruence

Congruence means being oneself. It implies genuineness and honesty with oneself when functioning as a counsellor. The counsellor does not pretend to be somebody he/she is not as this may bring about inconsistency. For example, it would not be helpful for a counsellor to be a "know it all" person or pretend to know something when in fact not. When he/she is unable to handle a situation, it is ideal to make a referral to others who may be in a position to effectively handle it. Inconsistency may lead to the client losing interest and confidence in the counsellor and consequently, the whole counselling process crumbling. It requires the counsellor`s ability to be open and honest and not to act in a superior manner or behind a professional façade (Doyle, 1992).

Positive Regard

Acceptance and respect for the client are essentials of the counselling relationship. The counsellor has to have regard for all clients regardless of their status in society. Moreover, the client's concerns should not be undervalued. Attention has to be paid to every concern or problem raised by the client. It involves showing the client that they are valued, regardless of who they are. The counsellor must be non-judgemental, accepting whatever the client says or does, without imposing values ((HIV/AIDS Counselling, 2001).

It is therefore, important for every counsellor to be acquainted with the basic counselling skills to aid the flow of the conversation, gain and clarify information from the client and show the client that he or she is being heard by exhibiting both the verbal and non-verbal ques. It is also important for the counsellor to refer cases or questions they cannot handle to other people. The skilled counsellor accepts all clients regardless of the living conditions.

What matters among other factors in the counselling process is to have regard for clients because they are human beings and acknowledging as well as, recognising their abilities and capabilities to solve their own problems as the counsellor facilitates the process.

CHAPTER 4

ETHICAL ISSUES IN COUNSELLING

Effective counselling requires the knowledge of counselling ethics, legal responsibilities and moral realities of living. Ethical issues for the counsellor include the necessity of understanding one's own motivation for entering the helping profession and one's responsibility to be aware of his or her own personal issues and to seek assistance when necessary. Counsellors have a further ethical responsibility to maintain high levels of professional competence in the areas of professional growth, accurate representation of services and training to clients and developing knowledge and expertise in specialised areas. Counsellors should ensure that they provide only those services and interventions for which they have adequate training (Van Niekerk and Prins, 2001). Counsellors or anyone involved in counselling should practise high levels of confidentiality, professional competence and be in a position to provide appropriate information to the clients for them to make their own choices.

Confidentiality

Confidentiality is the strongest expectation that clients have of counsellors in any given counselling relationship. Counsellors are expected to offer their clients the opportunity to express themselves and put across their problems without fear of possible disclosure to third parties. Counsellors are, by nature of their work, privy to the most personal and even intimate information about their clients. It is for this reason that they should regard all the information entrusted to them by the client as confidential unless both parties agree to disclose and to whom to disclose that information. Moreover, the counsellor needs to develop a sense of professional ethics for determining under which circumstances the confidentiality of the relationship should be broken.

According to Brown and Pate (1983) confidentiality is both an ethical and legal problem in counselling. Professional counsellors believe they have a right and in fact, a duty to safeguard information presented in a counselling interview. Clients, too, have a right to expect that information revealed to a counsellor will be held in strict confidence.

Professional Competence

One of the guiding ethical principles is that counsellors are expected to recognise their own personal and professional limitations. Professional competence not only focuses upon the quality of provided services, but also on boundaries of professional activity. Competent counsellors in the ethical sense are those counsellors who are capable of providing a minimum quality of service and that the service provided is clearly within the limits of the counsellor's training experience and practice as defined in professional standards. Counsellors who become aware of their lack of competence in a particular case have the responsibility to consult with colleagues (Core, 1993 in Van Niekerk and Prins, 2001).

Informed Consent

In the counselling relationship or process, the counsellor gives relevant information to the client after which the client is left to make a choice. This also applies in situations where a counsellor may need to transfer information about the client to a third party such as a lawyer, teacher, doctor or even another counsellor. Before the counsellor could transfer this confidential and private information, he or she must check with the client that he or she clearly understands the implications of the reasons for possible consequences of the disclosure. Only when the client gives consent should the counsellor disclose information (HIV/AIDS Counselling, 2001).

Maintaining ethical standards is what governs professions. A counsellor is required to hold in confidence every information that is entrusted to him or her by the client. He or She needs to work within the professional limitations and not going beyond, because in counselling one is dealing with the human mind which can be destroyed by wrong information.

It is also important to give the necessary information to the client so that they make their own choices based on the given information.

CHAPTER 5

APPROACHES TO COUNSELLING

There are many approaches used in counselling. Some counsellors use only one approach while others use techniques from more than one method. Before one starts counselling he or she should decide on the approach/ approaches to use. Or may decide to use techniques from other models if need be. These models just give guidance on how to go about counselling so that the counselling process is carried out in a systematic way. This chapter shall discuss the psychoanalytic, Humanistic, client centred and the behavioural approaches to counselling.

Psychoanalytic Approach to Counselling

Psychoanalytic counselling evolved from the work of Sigmund Freud. In his career as a medical doctor, Freud came across many patients who suffered from medical conditions which appeared to have no physical cause. This led him to believe that the origin of such illnesses lay in the conscious mind of the patient. He investigated the unconscious mind in order to understand his patients and assist in their healing. This approach is based on an individual's unconscious thoughts and perceptions that have developed throughout their childhood and how these affect their current behaviour and thoughts (Corey 1986). Feelings or emotions of grief, anger, and sadness may hinder survivorship if not dealt with. This knowledge is helpful in counselling patients suffering from cancer; an illness that has an impact on the minds of victims. It means that if the mind is not treated, optimal treatment cannot be achieved and patients' survival rates would be shortened. Psychoanalysis is used to encourage the client to examine their minds to gain a deeper understanding of themselves. This in turn may help the client to release negativities that they hold, associated with cancer and any other event in life that could worsen the situation. Psychoanalysis is based upon the assumption that only by becoming aware of earlier dilemmas, which have been repressed into our unconscious because of painful associations, can progress be made psychologically (Online Counselling Service, 2016).

Humanistic Approach to Counselling

Humanistic counselling recognises the uniqueness of every individual. Humanistic counselling assumes that everyone has an innate capacity to grow emotionally and psychologically towards the goal of self-actualisation and personal fulfilment. Humanistic counsellors work with the belief that it is not life events that cause problems, but how the individual experiences life events. How we experience life events will in turn relate to how we feel about ourselves; influencing self-esteem and confidence (Online Counselling Service, 2016). The counsellor using this approach, helps the client experience the cancer disease situation in a positive way by reminding them that they are still in control of their lives and that they are the only ones who can change the situation. It is also important to give the necessary information and assurance that the oncologists are available to treat, control or give the best supportive care depending on the stage of the disease and that the client has a part to play as well. The counsellor need to motivate the client so as to stir their self-esteem and confidence to handle their condition.

The humanistic approach to counselling encourages the client to learn to understand how negative responses to life can lead to psychological discomfort. The approach aims for acceptance of both the negative and positive aspects of oneself. Humanistic counsellors aim to help clients to explore their own thoughts and feelings and to work out their own solutions to their problems (Online Counselling Service, 2016).

Client Centred Counselling

The American psychologist, Carl Rogers (1902 – 1987) developed one of the most commonly used humanistic therapies, client centred counselling, which encourages the client to concentrate on how they feel at the present moment. The central theme of client centred counselling is the belief that we all have inherent resources that enable us to deal with whatever life brings (Doyle, 1992). In the case of cancer, it can be hope and the will power that can enable one to live a normal life even with a cancer diagnosis. Client centred therapy focuses on the belief that the client and not the counsellor is the best expert on their own thoughts, feelings, experiences and problems. It is, therefore, the client who is most capable of finding the most appropriate solutions. The counsellor's duty is to give information according to the identified gaps and let the client make their own choices.

The responsibility for working out problems rests wholly with the client. When the counsellor does respond, their aim is to reflect and clarify what the patient has been saying (Doyle, 1992). A trained client centred counsellor aims to show empathy, warmth and genuineness, which they believe will enable the client's self-understanding and psychological growth thereby giving hope to the patient.

Behavioural Approach to Counselling

Behavioural therapies are based on the way one thinks or behaves. It is based on observable behaviour. It recognises that it is possible to change or recondition thoughts or behaviour to overcome specific problems (Online Counselling Service 2016). How an individual responds to a given situation is due to behaviour that has been reinforced as a child. Behavioural therapies evolved from psychological research and theories of learning concerned with observable behaviour that is behaviour that can be objectively viewed and measured. Behaviourists believe that behaviour is learned and therefore, it can be unlearned. According to this approach unwanted behaviour is an undesired response to something or someone in a person's environment. Using this approach, a counsellor would identify the unwanted behaviour with a client and together they would work to change or modify the behaviour. Once the unwanted behaviour is identified, the client and counsellor might continue the process by drawing up an action plan of realistic, attainable goals. The aim would be that the unwanted behaviour stops altogether or is changed in such a way that it is no longer a problem (Van Niekerk and Prin 2001).

Behavioural counsellors or therapists use a range of behaviour modification techniques. The methods and procedures of behavioural counselling are based on social-learning theories - theories about how people learn and change their behaviour. Forms of learning, such as operant conditioning, classical conditioning, modelling, and cognitive processes, are used to help persons counselled change unwanted behaviour, and/or develop new, productive behaviour (UNESCO, 1998). Clients might be taught skills to help them manage their lives more effectively. For example, they may be taught how to adopt positive thoughts about cancer, like taking their life with cancer as a new normal, planning for the future of their loved ones (will writing) which others do not do and setting realistic goals. They are rewarded or positively reinforced when desirable behaviour occurs.

The reward can be in form of praise or compliments. Another method used involves learning desirable behaviour by watching and copying others who already behave in the desired way; like other cancer survivors. In general, the behavioural approach is concerned with the outcome rather than the process of change. The behavioural counsellor uses the skills of listening; reflection and clarification, to enable him or her make an assessment of all the factors relating to the undesirable behaviour.

All in all, there are so many counselling approaches that can be used to counsel cancer patients. It is up to the counsellor to choose the one that best suits. Approaches guide the counsellors in counselling so that they conduct the sessions in a systematic way.

CHAPTER 6

PROCESS OF COUNSELLING CANCER PATIENTS

As already mentioned, counselling is a process through which a client is helped to develop a better understanding of themselves, including their thought patterns, feelings, and behaviours, and the ways in which these may have been problematic in their lives and explore ways of dealing with such problems or feelings. Most importantly, the counsellor needs to know that the aim of counselling cancer patients is to help patients accept the illness and help reduce the burden so that people remain hopeful, functional and useful even in the face of an illness like cancer by providing all the necessary information about cancer and addressing the challenges as presented by the patients during counselling. It should be emphasised that counselling is not advice giving, but the provision of information for the patient to adopt what best suits them. It is unethical in counselling to advice the client but give enough and necessary information for them to decide their own course of action. The solutions to their problems should come from themselves after examining various options with the counsellor as a facilitator. The counsellor needs to choose the suitable approach to use from the ones given above or others that they may be privy to. All the counselling skills outlined above have to be utilised whenever necessary throughout the counselling process bearing in mind the ethical issues.

There are three possible ways by which clients seek counselling. They either go as self-referrals; or as invited by counsellors while, others are referred by health workers, family, friends and teachers. If the patient/client is not willing to be counselled, an appointment can be rescheduled. Patients should not be forced into counselling otherwise, it will be futile. Counselling is for the patient's benefit as such their full participation is important for them to deal with their situation.

Initial Contact

To start with, the counsellor welcomes the client with a smile in the counselling room and he or she introduces him or herself and then asks the client to do the same. The counselling room should be away from noise, well ventilated and comfortable for the client. A contract is made in which the counsellor and the client agree on the terms of reference. Assurance of confidentiality and privacy are some of the issues included in the contract.

- **Client's knowledge about cancer**

A further question may be asked of the client regarding their knowledge about cancer. The counsellor may then give more information about cancer in terms of what it is, the causes and available treatment modalities as well as the side effects. The counsellor should provide the information about how to deal with side effects or refer the patient to the nurses if need be. The client's initial concern or reason for seeking counselling should then be addressed. As the process goes on the counsellor, will discover other areas of concern which the client could not have mentioned initially and address them.

The counsellor has to bear this in mind that;

- Having cancer entails beginning a new life with a lot of adjustments to be made. It requires constant reviews and counselling and taking extra care of one self psychologically, physically and socially. Hence the patient needs to be told about what their new normal is, and life beyond the diagnosis. Many people are able to explore ways to cope with their diagnosis, manage any emotional concerns such as depression, anxiety, anger and confusion that may result after receiving news of their illness and discuss ways to address and cope with any life changes that may occur during the treatment process (National Cancer Institute, 2014).

- Those with families may experience distress over sharing the news with a partner or spouse and children. In this case, family counselling may be beneficial in helping the family members of those diagnosed with cancer learn ways to manage the varied emotions they may feel, such as anger, sadness, stress and grief. Partners, spouses and children may also be able to learn how to better support the member of the family who has cancer and family members can address any areas of conflict, which may be more likely to arise in a difficult time.

- **Followup counselling**

Counselling cancer patients should not be a one day session, but on going until, the desired outcome is achieved. Even then, when there are new developments like a recurrence of the disease or advancement of the disease, or any other pressing issue, the client is free to approach the counsellor. After the initial contact with the client, other dates can be set for them to meet again. During follow-ups, the counsellor needs to assess the impact of the previous counselling sessions by asking the client a few questions. If there be need a reinforcement is made by repeating whatever was discussed, if not they can proceed and talk about other emerging issues or the client can be discharged until such a time that he or she will be in need of counselling again.

There are main areas of concern that the counsellor needs to know about when counselling cancer patients. These are fear of stigma from the family and the community, recurrence of the disease and death. Giving hope to cancer patients is as well cardinal in counselling.

Main Areas of Concern in Counselling Cancer Patients

Working at the Cancer Diseases Hospital for five years as a Social Worker has helped the author to know some of the fears, worries and concerns that patients with cancer go through upon being diagnosed. Some patients become isolated and do not want to talk about their condition. Others start contemplating suicide. To make matters worse some patients face rejection from their spouses and family members. What brings all this is the fear of death, recurrence and stigma. Cancer patients are never free of thoughts of dying any time, or the disease coming back again and the stigma from the people around.

- **Fear of Stigma**

The cancer disease carries stigma. Despite treatment advances and extended survival rates for many cancers, cancer remains a stigmatised disease, and persons with cancer contend with societal attitudes, prejudices and discrimination on the basis of cancer history. Some people may change their attitudes towards a cancer patient. They may negatively stereotype the case and only see death when they see a cancer patient. Also due to lack of understanding, ignorance or fear about cancer, individuals with cancer or cancer survivors may face problems in getting employed or any promotion at the place for fear of losing out when the person dies. They believe cancer is an automatic death sentence (National Coalition for Cancer Survivors, 2015). This could be the reason why some patients are closed up; not wanting people to know they have cancer.

To deal with the stigma, the patient has to first accept they have cancer and gain an understanding into how society looks at cancer through counselling. Those who are able can open up and tell others about the disease. Once the patient has understood his or her situation then it will be easy to deal with others. Furthermore, those facing discrimination can be advised or connected to the human rights commission for support and other relevant authorities.

- **Fear of a Recurrence**

Research has indicated that reactions to the fear of recurrence of cancer range from worry, anger in the middle of the night to panic and thoughts of suicide. Insufficient knowledge of when symptoms will recur can significantly affect an individual's overall sense of control. A widely held assumption about recurrence is that an individual's response to recurrence is more distressing than the shock of the initial diagnosis. However some researchers have found that persons with a history of cancer already have developed some cancer related coping mechanisms (National Coalition for Cancer Survivorship, 2015). It is a fact from experience that most cancer patients dread a recurrence considering what they have to go through again like the side effects of treatment and the fear that death may be too close now. It is important initially, to tell the patient the treatment intent and the possibility of a recurrence and what they should expect. It is important for the counsellor to talk about recurrences in general before it occurs to prepare the client, so that even when it comes they will stand it using the strength and skills they will have acquired.

- **Fear of Death**

Dealing with the fear of death is not as easy as one may think. It brings thoughts of giving up, losing everything that one has worked for so hard, killing one's goals or cutting short one's life. Questions like; who will take care of my children come in, what will happen to my spouse if am gone? What will become of my children or my business? Why did I go to school if this is the end of it all? For those who do not believe in God it will be a question of where they will be when they die? Researchers in psychosocial oncology acknowledge that fear of death is a problem faced by persons diagnosed with cancer. Some researchers report that fear of death diminish the further away from the diagnosis period a person gets. While others report that fear of death may persist for years after cancer therapy is complete. Yet still other researchers note that even after what may be considered a definitive cure, survivors are less certain about living a long life. (National Coalition for Cancer Survivorship, 2015). Thoughts of death make an individual depressed, feel rejected, isolated, worthless and think that life is not worth living. A skilled counsellor will have this understanding even if the client does not declare they fear death. Some clients will come out bluntly and say like one woman "Ifwe nomba ku fwafye" (My time to die has come). When a client utters such words, it does not mean they are ready; they are looking for comfort and hope from you as a counsellor because they are hopeless. What hope does one give? False hope is not encouraged as the client will come back to you that you told them lies. It is very helpful in counselling patients to label the horror of the patient not knowing whether they are going to live or die as a real problem, as perhaps the worst problem involved with cancer, and point out that the medical team is ready to do what it can until time gives the answer (National Coalition for Cancer Survivorship, 2015). It is very disheartening to say that there is nothing that can be done to help the patient with cancer even in cases where the cancer has advanced. The fact should be communicated to the patient but an assurance of offering the best supportive care should also be given.

To help allay the fear of death; the counsellor needs to ask the client what they know about death and what brings about death. In the process they will realise that everyone will die and that death is a natural and common happening to all humanity like another client said that "no one is immune to death". The difference is that people die at different times with different causes. Some die suddenly while for others it is as result of chronic illnesses like cancer. Moreover, there are cancer patients who have lived longer than expected and there are individuals who have died sooner than the cancer patients. What matters is having a positive outlook of the whole situation. This realisation may not come in one counselling session for some clients; it can take more than one counselling session for them to come to this realisation. This calls for patience on the part of the counsellor. Once the client has realised that; the counsellor can remind the client that they are still alive and so can still make a difference in society as time and health allows.

Ask the client what he or she would want to achieve in life or see happen to his or her children/ spouse/ business/ company and how they would go about achieving it and encourage them to work towards that with a positive mind. If they are Christians encourage them to pray. If they are not; ask them if they would want to become Christians and connect them to pastors or priests. Most patients who have faith in the God of Israel find it easier to deal with the fear of death as they put their trust in Him (Romans chapter 10 verse 9 to 11). With permission from the patient; involve the family throughout so that they are also helped as they may be going through the same fears and pain as their loved one.

• **Giving Hope**

Hope is what makes a cancer patient remain positive. This should be known by every person counselling or dealing with a cancer patient if they have to help them remain positive throughout the diagnosis, treatment and survivorship. Cancer patients as well as survivors need and desire accurate and honest information about their disease, treatment, potential side effects and prognosis. What matters is how the information is presented because if presented with compassion and with assurance for continued support, even bad news can be accepted and new and more realistic goals can be assimilated into the hope process (National Coalition for Cancer survivorship, 2015)

For the individual and the family, cancer has a profound negative impact, yet hopefulness and a positive future orientation are important components for better quality of life in cancer survivorship. According to the National Coalition for Cancer survivorship (2015) hope is a complex concept that often is misunderstood by many people including health care professionals. Because they tend to think in terms of therapeutic hope which is hope based on therapy and is related to a cure or remission of disease. There is hope to maintain a high quality of life despite a cancer diagnosis.

Hope is a way of thinking, feeling and acting. It is in fact a prerequisite for action. Hope is flexible, and it remains open to various possibilities and the necessity to change the desired outcome as the reality changes. These aspects of hope emphasise how important hope is for living with an illness as serious as cancer. It is a phenomenologically positive state, and as such hope can never be false.

In his book Anatomy of hope, Groopman (2004) states that there is an authentic biology of hope and that belief and expectation are key elements of hope. It is necessary for healthy coping; its key purposes being the avoidance of despair and desire to make life under stress bearable. It is a cognitive affective resource that is a psychological asset. Its importance becomes greater in times of threat. Hope means desirability of personal survival and the ability of an individual to exert a degree of influence on the surrounding world.

Hope is not a static concept. It changes as situations and circumstances change. For example, when a cancer diagnosis is first determined, an individual almost hopes for complete cure. If this is not possible, that hope may be transformed into hope for long-term control of the disease, or for extended periods between recurrences. Even when hope for survival is dim, individuals will find other things to hope for like to see a grandchild born, control of pain or even a dignified death (National Coalition for Cancer Survivorship, 2015).

Maintaining this hope is not always easy and at times of crises, one may need additional support and encouragement from family, health care team, a counsellor and other cancer survivors. It is not time for false assurances, but instead, it requires helping to evaluate the situation realistically and to refocus hope. It is clear that hope functions as a protective mechanism, while hopelessness threatens physical, psychosocial and spiritual health and quality of life.

According to the National Cancer Institute (2012) one can feel a sense of hope, despite the cancer. But what is hoped for changes with time. If one is told that remission may not be possible, one can hope for other things. These may include comfort, peace, acceptance, and even joy. Hoping may give you a sense of purpose. This, in itself, may help one feel better.

- **How to build a sense of hope in clients**

To build a sense of hope, help the client to set goals to look forward to each day. Help them plan something to get their minds off cancer. Plan their day as they have always done; they should not stop doing the things they like to do just because they have cancer. Ask them to find small things in life to look forward to each day; set dates and events to look forward to. They should not limit themselves but look for reasons to hope while staying aware of what`s at hand (National Cancer Institute, 2014). Let them know that Doctors are there to help them treat and control the cancer as well as to manage the symptoms so that they live a more satisfying life and without pain even in the face of a cancer disease. Counsellors are called to help clients to be hopeful despite having cancer. This can be applied even in other life limiting conditions as well as chronic illnesses.

Referral to other Resources

Whenever, necessary, the client can be referred to other resource persons or Non-Governmental Organisations depending on their needs. Support groups also help in bringing persons with cancer together to share their experiences and encourage one another to fight on and never to lose hope. Furthermore, the client may be referred back to an oncologist, oncology nurse or the nutritionist if need be and the Palliative care team for further management. In an oncology centre, health workers work as a team for the benefit of the client. Each member has a role to play hence, the need for referrals.

Truth of the Matter

The truth of the matter is that there are multiple types of cancer, many of which can today be effectively treated so as to eliminate, reduce or slow the impact of the disease on patients' lives; coupled with counselling which helps to heal the mind. More people with cancer are not only surviving; they are living longer than was possible because of counselling. Weller, a counsellor says she talks with cancer patients about what their new normal is, and life beyond the diagnosis. Patients go through it and normalise their whole lives (Docksai, 2015). Therefore, counselling is an important component in the treatment of cancer patients without which survivorship could be shortened.

REFERENCES

American Cancer Society, (2011). *Cancer in Africa.* Atlanta: American Cancer Society.

Burchell, C. R. (1977). Extracted from the Audio-Digest Obstetrics and Gynaecology, Vol. 23, No. 14.

Brown, J. A. and Pate, R. H. (1983). Being A Counsellor: Directions and Challenges. California: Brooks/Cole.

Corey, G. (1986). *Case Approach to Counselling and Psychotherapy.* California: Brooks/Cole.

Donkor, A. (2015). Factors contributing to late presentation of Breast cancer in Africa: A systematic literature review. *Arch Med.* Vol. 8 No2.2

Doyle, R. E. (1992). *Essential Skills and Strategies in the Helping Process.* California: Brooks/Cole.

Egan, G. (1994). *The skilled helper: The Problem – Management Approach to Helping* (5th Ed). California: Brooks/Cole.

Groopman, J. (2004). *Anatomy of Hope- How People Prevail in the Face of Illness.* New York: Rando House.

Jemal, A., Bray, F., Forman, D., Ferlay, J., Center, M., O'Brien, M. and Parkin, M. (2012). Cancer burden in Africa and opportunities for prevention. *Cancer in Africa.* Sept 5, 2012.

Faiber, J. M., Weinerman, B. H. and Kuypers, J. A. (1985). Psychosocial Distress in Oncology out Patients. *Journal of Psychosocial Oncology, 2(314), 109-18.*

UNESCO, (1998). Counselling module 2: A paper presented to the Regional Training Seminar on Guidance and Counselling, April, 1998.

Van Niekerk, E. and Prins, A. (2001). *Counselling in Southern African: A youth Perspective.* Heineman: Bloemfontein.

Zambia Counselling Council, (1999). *Code of Ethics and Practise for Counselling in Zambia.* Lusaka, Zambia: University of Zambia press.

Zambia National Cancer Registry, (2012). *Cancer Registration 2008 – 2012.* Lusaka, Zambia.

Zondervan, (2000). *New International Standard Version Bible.* Colorado, United States of America: Zondervan.

American Cancer Society, (2015). *Facts about Cancer Pain.* Available at: http://www.cancer.org/treatment/treatmentandsideeffects/pyhsicalsideeffects/pain/fac. Accessed on: 30/03/2016.

American Cancer Society, (2015). *What are the Goals of Chemotherapy as Cancer Treatment.* Available at http://www.cancer.org/treatment/treatmentsideeffects/treatmenttypes/chemotherapy/chemoth erapy-goals. Accessed on: 21/01/2016.

Cancer Research UK, (2014). *How Cancer Starts.* Available at: http://www.cancerresearchuk.org/about-cancer/what-is-cancer/how-cancer-starts. Accessed on: 03/01/2016.

Docksai, R. *Cancer – Patient Counsellor Saundra Weller Hepls Patients Live Life after Treatment.* Available at: http://www.counselor-licence.com/articles/cancer-counselor-weller.html. Accessed on: 19/08/2015.

Evert, J. (2010). *Overview: Introduction to Cancer.* Available at: http://www.mentalhelp.net/articles/overview-introduction-to-cancer/ Accessed on: 22/01/2016.

Hejmadi, M. (2014). *How Cancer Arises.* Available at: http://www.futurelearn.com/courses/inside-cancer-2014-q3. Accessed on: 13/10/205.

Moyinham, T. (2014). *Cancer pain: relief is possible.* Available at: http://www.mayoclinic.org/diseases-conditions/ cancer/indepth/cancer-pain/art-   20045118. Accessed on:30/03/2016.

National Cancer Institute, (2015). *Risk Factors for Cancer.* Available at: http://www.cancer.gov/about-cancer/ causes-prevention/risk. Accessed on: 26/08/2015.

National Cancer Institute, (2015). *What is cancer?* Available at: http://www.cancer.gov/about-cancer/what-is-cancer. Accessed on: 13/10/2015.

National Cancer Institute, (2015). *Radiation Therapy for Cancer.* Available at: http://www.cancer.gov/about-cancer/treatment/types/radiation-therapy/radiation-fact- sheet. Accessed on: 21/01/2016.

National Cancer Institute (2015). *Side Effects of Cancer Treatment.* Available at: http://www.cancer.gov/ about-cancer/treatment/side-effects. Accessed on: 11/10/2015.

National Cancer Institute, (2014). Coping- *Feelings and Cancer.* Available at: http://www.cancer.gov/about-cancer/coping/feelings. Accessed on: 11/10/2015.

National Coalition for Cancer Survivorship. *Cancer and Fear.* Available at: http://www.cancer advocacy. org/resources/remaining-hopeful/cancer-and-fear/ Accessed on: 24/02/2016.

National Coalition for Cancer Survivorship. *Remaining Positive.* Available at: http://www.canceradvocacy.org/resources/remaining-hopeful/remaining-positive/ Accessed on: 24/02/2016.

The Online Counselling Service (2016). *Methods, Models And Approaches To Counselling And Psychotherapy.* Available at: http://www.onlinecounsellingservice.co.uk/therapy- methods. Accessed on: 10/03/2016.

CPSIA information can be obtained
at www.ICGtesting.com
Printed in the USA
LVOW07s2130030617
536844LV00001B/6/P